LEOPARDS

Sandie Lee Books

Leopards

Leopards are a part of the cat family called, Felidae. The scientific name for this animal is Panthera pardus. They are called, Chui in Swahili. Leopards are not the biggest in the cat family, but they are built for hunting. Although, they will hunt humans, this only happens when the animal is stressed or injured. Let's take a tour around the world of the leopard to see what other cool facts we can "spot." Check it out...

Where in the World?

Did you know leopards like the cover of dense bush and rocky areas to live in? The number of leopards in the world is declining. They were once found in several areas, but now are mostly located in sub-Saharan Africa. Smaller groups are also living in India, China, Pakistan, Indochina and Malaysia.

The Body of a Leopard

Did you know the leopard is very powerful? This cat weighs about 140 pounds as an adult. It has a long tail it uses for balance when it is in the trees and short, stocky legs. Its head is broad with ears that stand erect. The eyes of the leopard can be pale green to gray in color.

The Coat of a Leopard

Did you know the leopard's coat can be different colors, depending on it where it lives? Leopards that live in grasslands have light yellow coats with black spots and rosettes. Leopards that are found in forests tend to be darker with more markings. This is known as camouflage and let's the leopard remain unseen.

What a Leopard Eats

Did you know leopards are carnivores? This meat-eating cat will hunt larger prey like deer and warthogs. But when these animals are not available, the leopard will hunt for birds, small mammals, reptiles and even dung beetles. This cat only hunts when it is hungry and has to avoid tigers and hyenas when it has made a kill.

The Leopard's Special Ability

Did you know the leopard is a great climber? The leopard spends a lot of its time in the trees. It has powerful and strong front legs that help it climb. This cat also has very sharp claws that are retractable. This means they can pull them back into their paws when not in use.

The Leopard as a Predator

Did you know the leopard is a stealthy hunter? Leopards are mostly nocturnal. This means they do most of their hunting at night. After a leopard has made a kill, it will drag it up into a tree to eat. It will eat until it is full, then leave the rest in the tree for later.

The Leopard as Prey

Did you know leopard cubs are hunted by tigers and hyenas? Man also poses a threat to the leopard. This cat is poached for its coat and also its body parts. Some cultures believe the leopard's whiskers and bones have healing properties. This has led to many leopards being killed. It is now considered endangered.

The Leopard Territory

Did you know leopards like to live alone? Male leopards do not like to share their territory with other males, but they will share it with females. The male will scent mark its area by urinating on objects like trees and rocks. The male will also use its sharp claws to scratch trees. This tells other males to "back off!"

Leopard Talk

Did you know leopards can communicate? An angry leopard will growl, spit and make a screaming roar. When a male is marking his territory he will make a raspy or sawing, cough-like sound. A leopard that is happy and content will purr. Mom leopard will lick and also purr to her kittens.

The Leopard Mom

Did you know the female leopard leaves a scent trail for the male? A female leopard gives off a scent and will rub trees to leave her smell there. She will also make a special call to the males in the area. After the female has mated she will give birth to 2 to 6 babies.

The Leopard Baby

Did you know baby leopards are called cubs? Leopard cubs are born only weighing about 1 pound. Their coats are very fuzzy with blurry markings. They drink milk from their mother until they are about 3 months old. The cubs stay with their mother until they are about 18 months old.

Leopards at Rest

Did you know leopards like to sleep high up in the trees? Even though leopards only stay in one spot for a few days at a time, they still have to rest. Leopards will climb tall trees and lay out on a thick branch. From here it will rest, sleep and even watch for prey.

Life of a Leopard

Did you know leopards can live from 12 to 17 years in the wild? Because some baby leopards fall prey to tigers and hyenas, not all of them make it to adulthood. However, the ones that do can live a full life. Leopards in zoos can live to be upwards of 21 years-old.

Snow Leopards

This type of leopard is found in the mountains of central Asia. Its coat is silvery in color with dark spots and rosettes. It has extra-large paws that keep it from sinking into the snow. This cat can grow to be about 120 pounds and is very strong and powerful.

Quiz

Question 1: What does the leopard use its long tail for?

Answer 1: The tail helps balance the leopard when it is walking in the trees

Question 2: The leopard's claws are retractable. What does this allow it to do?

Answer 2: The leopard can pulls its claws into its feet.

Question 3: What does a leopard do with its kill before it eats it?

Answer 3: The leopard drags its kill up into a tree to keep it safe from other predators

Question 4: What does an angry leopard do?

Answer 4: It will spit, growl and make a screaming roar

Question 5: How long do baby leopards stay with their mom?

Answer 5: Babies are ready to leave their mom at around 18 months-old.

Thank you for checking out another addition from Sandie Lee Books! Make sure to check out Amazon.com for many other great titles.